The AOTA Practice Guidelines Series

Occupational Therapy
Practice Guidelines *for*

Home
Modifications

Carol Siebert, MS, OTR/L
In collaboration with the AOTA Commission on Practice

AOTA PRESS®
The American
Occupational Therapy
Association, Inc.

Vision Statement

AOTA advances occupational therapy as the pre-eminent profession in promoting the health, productivity, and quality of life of individuals and society through the therapeutic application of occupation.

Mission Statement

The American Occupational Therapy Association advances the quality, availability, use, and support of occupational therapy through standard-setting, advocacy, education, and research on behalf of its members and the public.

AOTA Staff

Frederick P. Somers, Executive Director
Christopher M. Bluhm, Chief Operating Officer
Audrey Rothstein, Director, Marketing and Communications

Maureen Peterson, OT, Chief Professional Affairs Officer
Deborah Lieberman, OT, Practice Associate

Chris Davis, Managing Editor, AOTA Press
Carrie Mercadante, Editorial Assistant

Robert A. Sacheli, Manager, Creative Services
Sarah E. Ely, Book Production Coordinator

Marge Wasson, Marketing Manager
Elizabeth Sarcia, Marketing Specialist

The American Occupational Therapy Association, Inc.
4720 Montgomery Lane
Bethesda, MD 20814
Phone: 301-652-AOTA (2682)
TDD: 800-377-8555
Fax: 301-652-7711
www.aota.org

To order: 1-877-404-AOTA (2682)

Disclaimers

This publication is designed to provide accurate and authoritative information in regard to the subject matter covered. It is sold or distributed with the understanding that the publisher is not engaged in rendering legal, accounting, or other professional service. If legal advice or other expert assistance is required, the services of a competent professional person should be sought.
—*From the Declaration of Principles jointly adopted by the American Bar Association and a Committee of Publishers and Associations*

It is the objective of the American Occupational Therapy Association to be a forum for free expression and interchange of ideas. The opinions expressed by the contributors to this work are their own and not necessarily those of the American Occupational Therapy Association.

ISBN: 1-56900-212-6
Library of Congress Control Number: 2005902807

Contents

Introduction

Purpose and Use of This Document 1

Domain and Process of Occupational Therapy 1

    Domain 1

    Process 2

What Are Home Modifications? 3

    Need for Home Modifications 5

    Effectiveness of Home Modifications 6

Occupational Therapy and Home Modifications

Occupational Therapy Process 11

    Referral 11

    Evaluation 12

    Intervention 13

    Intervention Approaches and Strategies 13

        Education and Consultation 13

        Education and Training 14

    Family and Caregiver Education 15

    Intervention Implementation 15

        Activities of Daily Living 16

        Instrumental Activities of Daily Living 18

        Education and Work 20

        Play and Leisure 21

Other Professionals Involved in Home Modification Implementation 21

    Architects and Interior Designers 21

    Contractors, Remodelers, and Tradespeople 22

    Volunteers and "Do-It-Yourselfers" 22

Intervention Review 23

Outcomes 23

Follow-up Services 23

Appendix A

    Glossary of Terms and Definitions, Homes for Life Coalition of Howard County, Maryland 25

Appendix B

    Principles of Universal Design and Application to Home Modifications 33

Appendix C
Selected 2004 CPT™ Billing Codes Applicable to Home Modification Practice 35

Appendix D
Preparation and Qualifications of Occupational Therapists and Occupational Therapy Assistants 37

References 39

Selected Reading 41

Introduction

Purpose and Use of This Document

Practice guidelines for health care professionals have been widely developed in response to the health care reform movement in the United States. Such guidelines can be useful for improving the quality of health care, enhancing consumer satisfaction, promoting appropriate use of health care services, and reducing costs. The American Occupational Therapy Association (AOTA), which represents more than 35,000 occupational therapists, occupational therapy assistants, and students of occupational therapy, is committed to providing information to support decision making that promotes a health care system that is of high quality, accessible to all, and affordable.

Using key concepts from the *Occupational Therapy Practice Framework: Domain and Process* (AOTA, 2002), this guideline provides an overview of the occupational therapy process when interventions are directed toward home modifications. It defines the occupational therapy process that occurs within the boundaries of acceptable practice. Note that these guidelines may not include all appropriate methods of service. There may be legitimate reasons for departing from the content of this publication, and the ultimate judgment regarding the appropriateness of any given procedure is made by an occupational therapist in light of a specific client's circumstances.

It is the intention of AOTA, through this publication, to help its members, as well as those who manage, fund, or set policy regarding occupational therapy services and home modification services. This guideline serves as a reference for designers, builders, consumers, social services providers, health care facility managers, managed care organizations, health care regulators, third-party payers, occupational therapists, and occupational therapy assistants. It defines the contribution that occupational therapists and occupational therapy assis-

tants make to the home modification process through evaluation, consultation, and training with clients or consumers who need home modifications.*

Domain and Process of Occupational Therapy

"Occupational therapists' and occupational therapy assistants' expertise lies in their knowledge of occupation and how engaging in occupations can be used to affect human performance and the effects of disease and disability" (AOTA, 2002, p. 610). In 2002, the AOTA Representative Assembly adopted the *Occupational Therapy Practice Framework: Domain and Process*. Informed by the pre-existing *Uniform Terminology for Occupational Therapy* (AOTA, 1979, 1989, 1994) and the World Health Organization's (WHO, 2001) *International Classification of Functioning, Disability, and Health (ICF)*, the *Framework* outlines the profession's domain and the process of how occupational therapy services are delivered within this domain. Table 1 compares terminology used in the *Framework* and *ICF* documents.

Domain

A profession's *domain* articulates its sphere of knowledge, societal contribution, and intellectual or scientific activity. The occupational therapy profession's domain centers on helping others participate in daily

---

*The *occupational therapist* is responsible for all aspects of occupational therapy service delivery and is accountable for the safety and effectiveness of the occupational therapy service delivery process. The *occupational therapy assistant* delivers occupational therapy services under the supervision of and in partnership with an occupational therapist. When the term *occupational therapy practitioner* is used in this document, it refers to both occupational therapists and occupational therapy assistants.

Table 1. Comparison of the *Occupational Therapy Practice Framework: Domain and Process* and the *International Classification of Functioning, Disability, and Health*

Framework Construct	Comparable *ICF* Construct
Occupations: "Activities . . . of everyday life, named, organized, given value and meaning by individuals and a culture. Occupation is everything people do to occupy themselves, including looking after themselves, . . . enjoying life, . . . and contributing to the social and economic fabric of their communities . . ." (Law, Polatajko, Baptiste, & Townsend, 1997, p. 32).	Not addressed.
Areas of occupation: Various kinds of life activities in which people engage, including the following categories: ADL, IADL education, work, play, leisure, and social participation.	**Activities and Participation** **Activities:** "Execution of a task or action by an individual" (WHO, 2001, p. 8). **Participation:** "Involvement in a life situation" (WHO, 2001, p. 8). Examples of both include learning, task demands (routines), communication, mobility, self-care, domestic life, interpersonal interactions and relationships, major life areas, community, social and civic life. Activities and Participation overlap Areas of Occupation, Performance Skills, and Performance Patterns in the *Framework*.
Performance skills: Features of what one does, not what one has, related to observable elements of action that have implicit functional purposes (adapted from Fisher & Kielhofner, 1995, p. 113). Performance skills include motor, process, and communication/interaction skills.	**Activities and Participation** **Activities:** "Execution of a task or action by an individual" (WHO, 2001, p. 8). **Participation:** "Involvement in a life situation" (WHO, 2001, p. 8). Examples of both include learning, task demands (routines), communication, mobility, self-care, domestic life, interpersonal interactions and relationships, major life areas, community, social and civic life. Activities and Participation overlap Areas of Occupation, Performance Skills, and Performance Patterns in the *Framework*.
Performance patterns: Patterns of behavior related to daily life activities that are habitual or routine. Performance patterns include habits, routines, and roles.	**Activities and Participation** **Activities:** "Execution of a task or action by an individual" (WHO, 2001, p. 8). **Participation:** "Involvement in a life situation" (WHO, 2001, p. 8). Examples of both include learning, task demands (routines), communication, mobility, self-care, domestic life, interpersonal interactions and relationships, major life areas, community, social and civic life. Activities and Participation overlap Areas of Occupation, Performance Skills, and Performance Patterns in the *Framework*.

(continued)

life activities. The broad term that the profession uses to describe daily life activities is *occupation*. As outlined in the *Framework*, occupational therapists and occupational therapy assistants work collaboratively with clients to promote engagement in occupation to support participation in contexts, regardless of the practice setting or population (see Figure 1). This overarching mission circumscribes the profession's domain and emphasizes the important ways in which the environment and life circumstances influence how people carry out their occupations. Key terms regarding the domain of occupational therapy are outlined in Table 2.

When home modifications are being addressed, many terms are used that are drawn from the design and construction arena, as well as concepts that are defined in laws related to accessibility. Some terms that are used in common parlance have specific meanings as they relate to home modifications (see Appendix A).

Process

Many professions use the *process* of evaluating, intervening, and targeting outcomes that is outlined in the *Framework* (AOTA, 2002). However, occupational therapy's focus on occupation makes the profession's

Framework Construct	Comparable ICF Construct
Context or Contexts: Refers to a variety of interrelated conditions within and surrounding the client that influence performance, including cultural, physical, social, personal, spiritual, temporal, and virtual contexts.	**Contextual Factors:** "Represent the complete background of an individual's life and living. They include environmental factors and personal factors that may have an effect on the individual with a health condition and the individual's health and health-related states" (WHO, 2001, p.14). **Environmental factors:** "Make up the physical, social, and attitudinal environment in which people live and conduct their lives. The factors are external to individuals . . ." (WHO, 2001, p.14). **Personal factors:** "The particular background of an individual's life and living . . ." (WHO, 2001, p.15; e.g., gender, race, lifestyle, social background, education, profession). Personal factors are not classified in ICF because they are not part of a health condition or health state, although they are recognized as having an effect on outcomes.
Activity demands: The aspects of an activity, which include the objects, social demands, sequencing or timing, required actions, and required underlying body functions and body structures, needed to carry out the activity.	Not addressed.

Client factors: Those factors that reside within the client that may affect performance in areas of occupation. Client factors include the following:
     Body functions: "The physiological functions of body systems (including psychological functions)" (WHO, 2001, p. 8).
     Body structures: "Anatomical parts of the body such as organs, limbs, and their components [that support body function]" (WHO, 2001, p. 8).
	Body functions: "The physiological functions of body systems (including psychological functions)" (WHO, 2001, p. 8).
	 Body structures: "Anatomical parts of the body such as organs, limbs, and their components [that support body function]" (WHO, 2001, p. 8).

Outcomes: Important dimensions of health attributed to interventions, including ability to function, health perceptions, and satisfaction with care (adapted from Request for Planning Ideas, 2001).	Not addressed.

Note. ICF = *International Classification of Functioning, Disability, and Health;* WHO = World Health Organization.
Adapted from American Occupational Therapy Association. (2002). Occupational therapy practice framework: Domain and process. *American Journal of Occupational Therapy, 56,* pp. 637–639.

application of this process unique (see Figure 2). The process of occupational therapy service delivery begins by evaluating the client's occupational needs, problems, and concerns and analyzing the performance skills, patterns, contexts, activity demands, and client factors that contribute to or impede the client's satisfaction with his or her ability to engage in valued daily life activities. Occupational therapists then use a variety of approaches and methods in which occupation is both means and ends (Trombly, 1995). Occupational therapists and occupational therapy assistants continually monitor the effectiveness of interventions and the progress toward targeted outcomes. Occupational ther-

apists select outcome measures that are valid, reliable, and appropriately sensitive to the client's occupational performance, satisfaction, adaptation, role competence, health and wellness, and quality of life. The intervention review informs recommendations to continue or discontinue intervention as well as referrals to other agencies or professionals.

What Are Home Modifications?

Home modifications are both product and process. A *home modification product* is defined as any alteration, adjustment, or addition to the home environment

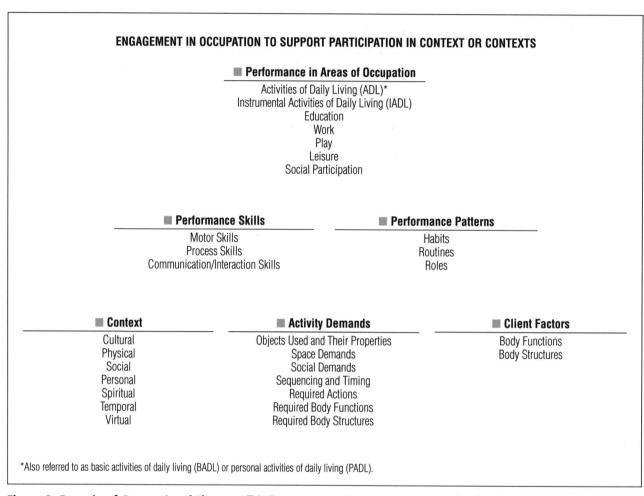

ENGAGEMENT IN OCCUPATION TO SUPPORT PARTICIPATION IN CONTEXT OR CONTEXTS

■ **Performance in Areas of Occupation**

Activities of Daily Living (ADL)*
Instrumental Activities of Daily Living (IADL)
Education
Work
Play
Leisure
Social Participation

■ **Performance Skills**

Motor Skills
Process Skills
Communication/Interaction Skills

■ **Performance Patterns**

Habits
Routines
Roles

■ **Context**

Cultural
Physical
Social
Personal
Spiritual
Temporal
Virtual

■ **Activity Demands**

Objects Used and Their Properties
Space Demands
Social Demands
Sequencing and Timing
Required Actions
Required Body Functions
Required Body Structures

■ **Client Factors**

Body Functions
Body Structures

*Also referred to as basic activities of daily living (BADL) or personal activities of daily living (PADL).

Figure 1. Domain of Occupational Therapy. This figure represents the domain of occupational therapy and is included to allow readers to visualize the entire domain with all of its various aspects. No aspect is intended to be perceived as more important than another.

Note. From American Occupational Therapy Association. (2002). Occupational therapy practice framework: Domain and process. *American Journal of Occupational Therapy, 56,* p. 611.

through the use of specialized, customized, off-the-shelf, or universally designed technologies, equipment, products, hardware, controls and cues, finishes, furnishings, and other features that affect the layout and structure to improve functional capability of or minimize environmental demands on individuals and their caregivers to meet the situational needs for promoting performance of daily activities as independently and safely as possible (adapted from Sanford, 2004). The *home modification process* is defined as the confluence of activities and delivery of services, including assessing needs, identifying solutions, implementing solutions, training in use of solutions, and evaluating outcomes, that contribute to any alteration, adjustment, or addition to the home environment through the use of specialized, customized, off-the-shelf, or universally designed technologies, equipment, products, hardware, controls and cues, finishes, furnishings, and other features that affect the layout and structure to improve functional capability of or minimize environmental demands on individuals and their caregivers to meet the situational needs for promoting performance of

Table 2. Key Terms in the *Occupational Therapy Practice Framework: Domain and Process*

Performance in Areas of Occupation: The broad range of life activities in which people engage, including

- Activities of daily living that are oriented to taking care of one's own body, such as bathing (Rogers & Holm, 1994);
- Instrumental activities that are oriented toward interacting with the environment, such as home management (Rogers & Holm, 1994);
- Education that incorporates activities needed for being a student and participating in a learning environment;
- Work activities needed for engaging in remunerative employment or volunteer activities (Mosey, 1996, p. 341);
- Play activities that provide enjoyment, amusement, or diversion (Parham & Fazio, 1997, p. 252);
- Leisure activities that people engage in during discretionary time (Parham & Fazio, 1997, p. 250);
- Social participation activities that involve interactions with community, family, and friends (adapted from Mosey, 1996, p. 340).

Performance skills: Features of what one does, not what one has, related to observable elements of action that have implicit functional purposes (Fisher & Kielhofner, 1995). Motor, process, and communication/interaction skills enable people to carry out occupations.

Performance patterns: Established modes of behavior related to habits, routines, and roles.

Context(s): The array of interrelated conditions within and surrounding an individual that influence performance, including cultural, physical, social, personal, spiritual, temporal, and virtual dimensions (AOTA, 2002).

Activity demands: The aspects of an activity, which include the objects, space, social demands, sequencing or timing, required actions, and required underlying body functions and body structure needed to carry out the activity (AOTA, 2002).

Client factors: Body structures and body functions that reside within the client and that may affect performance in areas of occupation (AOTA, 2002). Body structures are "the physiological functions of body systems (including psychological functions)" (WHO, 2001, p. 10).

Note. AOTA = American Occupational Therapy Association; WHO = World Health Organization.
Adapted from American Occupational Therapy Association. (2002). Occupational therapy practice framework: Domain and process. *American Journal of Occupational Therapy, 56*, 609–639.

daily activities as independently and safely as possible (adapted from Sanford, 2004). This guideline articulates the involvement of occupational therapy practitioners in the home modification *process.*

Occupational therapists and occupational therapy assistants define *occupational performance* as the ability to carry out activities of daily life: "Occupational performance is the outcome of the transaction of the person, environment, and occupation. It is defined as the dynamic experience of a person engaged in purposeful activities and tasks within an environment" (Law, Cooper, Strong, Stewart, Rigby, & Letts, 1996, p. 16). Occupational therapy practitioners bring this unique perspective to the home modification process. Occupational therapy focuses on the interaction of a client's skills and abilities, the features of the environment, and the demands and purposes of the activity. This interaction is more than one of ergonomics, which focuses primarily on effectiveness of "fit" between body

and device. For fit to be transformed into occupational engagement, factors such as satisfaction, safety, efficiency, and adequacy also must be considered. This dynamic person–environment–occupation transaction is addressed when occupational therapy is involved in the home modification process.

Need for Home Modifications

When the interaction between the client's abilities (performance skills, performance patterns) and the supports or challenges of the environment (activity demands; physical, cultural, or social context) is ineffective or disrupted, the need for home modifications may arise. The result of this disruption is that "too often, older or disabled people live limited lives or give up their homes and neighborhoods prematurely because standard housing of the past cannot meet their needs" (Mace, 1997, quoted in Center for Universal Design, 1997a, p. ix).

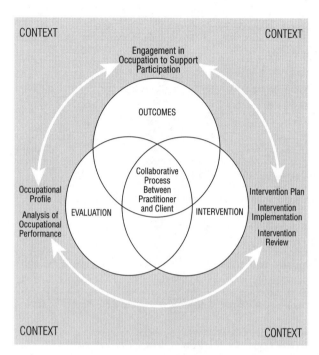

Figure 2. Framework Collaborative Process Model.
Illustration of the framework emphasizing client–practitioner
interactive relationship and interactive nature of the service
delivery process.

Note. From American Occupational Therapy Association. (2002). Occupational therapy practice framework: Domain and process. *American Journal
of Occupational Therapy, 56,* p. 614.

A nationwide survey of adults ages 45 and older
conducted by AARP (2000) examined their opinions
and behaviors regarding current and future housing
(see Table 3). Results suggest that the adult population
considers modification of the environment a desirable
strategy to support aging in place but also indicate that
this same population considers its knowledge of home
modification inadequate.

The AARP survey focused on home modifications
for safety and did not address home modifications to
support engagement in occupation or to reduce caregiving demands. While only 8 percent of respondents
identified a specific limitation in mobility affecting
themselves or a household member, a majority of
respondents (90%) have made modifications and, of
these, 67% expect that these changes will allow them
or others in the household to live in the home longer

than would be expected without the modification.
This survey indicates that individuals who are not currently experiencing difficulties in their daily activities
are nonetheless strongly interested in modifying the
home to sustain continued performance to allow the
individual to age in place.

Effectiveness of Home Modifications

Currently, there are no widely available outcome measures designed to gauge the effectiveness of home modifications. In many cases, home modifications are one
of many intervention strategies being considered, and
even when results are favorable, the contributions of
the various intervention strategies cannot be discretely
identified and quantified. In other cases, home modifications are a single intervention strategy, but the
method for identifying the effects of the modifications
is limited to a specific parameter, such as intensity of
physical assistance with specific tasks, and other effects
such as risk reduction, satisfaction, or caregiver burden
are not measured. The following section reports the
findings from various studies that have identified outcomes achieved through home modifications and,
where available, efforts to measure the effectiveness of
these.

One recent study examined the effects of removing
environmental barriers on the occupational performance of older adults (Stark, 2004). The Canadian
Occupational Performance Measure (Law, Baptiste,
Carswell, McColl, Polatajko, & Pollock, 1994) was
used to measure participants' occupational performance and satisfaction with performance. Although this
study was based on a very small sample, "all subjects
reported a positive change from before to after intervention with regard to their occupational performance.
. . . After receiving home modifications, participants
experienced statistically significant increase in both
participation and satisfaction scores" (Stark, 2004,
p. 37).

Most studies of home modification effectiveness
have been limited to the relationship of home modifications to falls or their prevention. It is significant that
the only studies that have associated home modifications with reduction in falls risk have included home

Table 3. Selected Responses to the AARP *Fixing to Stay* Survey

Survey Question or Topic	Responses
Would like to remain in current home as long as possible—strongly agree	71%
Would like to remain in current home as long as possible—somewhat agree	12%
If need help caring for self, prefer not to move from current home	82%
Respondent or a member of household has difficulty getting around in the home	8%
Respondents who expect that, within 5 years, they or a household member will experience problems getting around in the house	23%
Very or somewhat concerned about being able to provide care to a parent or relative	27%
Have made at least one simple change to the home to make it easier to live there (e.g., night-lights, nonskid strips in tub, higher wattage light bulbs, lever knobs on doors, secured carpets, lever faucet knobs, telephones with large-print keypad)	86%
If permitted, have made at least one major modification to the home to make it easier to live there (e.g., light switches at top and bottom of dark stairwells, bedroom/bath facilities on first floor, handrails on both sides of steps or stairs, grab bars or handrails in bathroom)	70%
Respondents who have made at least one modification (major or minor) to the home	90%
Of those who have made modifications, respondents who expect that the modifications will allow respondent or household member to live in the home longer than without modification	67%
Reason for making home modification—safety	70%
Reason for making home modification—easier to use for all household members	65%
Reason for not modifying home, or not modifying it as much as desired—not knowing how to make the changes	25%
Express interest in receiving information about staying in own home while aging	52%
Indicate interest in information about types of home modification	28%

Note. Adapted from AARP. (2000). *Fixing to stay: A national survey on housing and home modification issues.* Washington, DC: AARP, Independent Living Program.

visits by an occupational therapist to address the person–environment fit and to instruct participants in strategies and behaviors to incorporate the modifications during their daily activities. In a randomized, controlled trial conducted in Australia, a single visit by an occupational therapist was made to homes of older adults to assess and address environmental hazards (Cumming, Thomas, Szonyi, Frampton, Salkeld, & Clemson, 2001). During the visit, recommendations were made for specific changes in the environment, and instruction was provided in behavioral strategies related to the environment (e.g., leaving a light on at night to illuminate pathways). Recommendations were supported with resources to obtain or install the proposed modifications. The results indicated that, among older adults who had sustained a fall in the year before the study, the intervention reduced the risk of falling by 19% (Cumming et al., 1999).

A similar randomized, controlled trial was conducted in Great Britain using a multidisciplinary approach (Close, Ellis, Hooper, Glucksman, Jackson, & Swift, 1999). The participants were older adults who had sustained a fall and presented to an emergency or accident ward for care. Those in the intervention group underwent a single detailed medical assessment in a day hospital and a single detailed occupational therapy assessment in the home, whereas those in the control group received "usual care." The occupational therapist's visit entailed evaluation of performance in the environment and included environmental assessment and a falls hazard assessment. Intervention participants received follow-up services based on the medical assessment (e.g., modification of drug regimen), and minor modifications or assistive technology was provided to the participants based on the occupational therapy assessment. "Minor equipment was supplied directly by the occupational therapist" (p. 94). At 12-month follow-up, the total number of falls reported by the control group was more than 3 times greater than that reported by the intervention group. The risk of falling and the number of recurrent falls was decreased in the intervention group as compared to the control group. There also was more reported decline in performance of daily living skills in the control group than in the intervention group.

In contrast, a study of environmental intervention to prevent falls (Gill, Williams, & Tinetti, 2000) focused on home visits by nurses to assess the environment for falls using criteria commonly available in home safety or fall prevention checklists. No intervention was offered to modify the environment or alter the person–environment interaction. Falls outside the home or falls on stairs were excluded from the study results. Although the study authors concluded that "formal home safety assessment may not be a particularly effective strategy to prevent falls (p. 1180), an alternative conclusion might be that assessment of the environment alone (without assessing or addressing performance of occupations in that environment) is ineffective in preventing falls or improving safety in the home.

The AARP Public Policy Institute conducted an analysis of data on cost and incidence of falls in the home and the potential savings from home modifications (Kochera, 2002). This meta-analysis was inconclusive, in part because no consistent methodology exists for identifying or implementing home modifica-

tions, for determining fall reduction, or for calculation of cost savings when research in this area has been conducted. Most significantly, current research on falls prevention and home modification has focused on the presence or absence of falls and the presence or absence of specified modifications but has not focused on participants' interaction with the environment in the course of performing daily occupations. The summary stated that "more comprehensive research that includes detailed information on residents and home features, with a large sample size to adequately test the statistical significance of various factors, is clearly warranted" (p. 12).

While prevention of falls is most often identified as a rationale for home modifications, there also are outcomes related to occupational engagement and reduction of caregiver burden and health care costs. Outcomes related to these factors are supported by an abundance of anecdotal evidence, but several studies have examined these outcomes as a function of home modification. A study of the effectiveness of environmental interventions and assistive technology for frail elders (Mann, Ottenbacher, Fraas, Tomita, & Granger, 1999) measured effectiveness of these interventions in multiple domains. The Functional Independence Measure (FIM; Center for Functional Assessment Research/Uniform Data System for Medical Rehabilitation, 1984) was used to assess changes in overall performance and motor function. The study also used health care costs as a measure of the effectiveness of the interventions. In this randomized, controlled trial, the intervention strategy included a

Comprehensive functional assessment of the person and the home by an occupational therapist, recommendations for needed assistive devices and/or home modifications (designated by the investigators as AT [assistive technology] and EI [environmental intervention], provision of the devices and modifications, training in their use, and continued follow-up with assessment and provision of AT–EIs as needs changed. (p. 211)

Results of the study indicate that, while FIM scores declined for both AT–EI recipients and the control group, there was significantly more decline in the control group. The control group also experienced significantly more pain at the end of the 18-month intervention period. In addition, the control group required significantly more expenditures for institutional care over the study period as well as greater expenditures for nurse visits and case manager visits to the home.

This study also identified two measures for assessing outcomes associated with environmental modifications: (1) reduction in caregiving or assistance costs and (2) reduction in caregiving or assistance needs. Caregiving cost can be measured in terms of dollars spent for assistance per day or per week. Caregiving need can be measured both by intensity of assistance (e.g., "hands-on" assistance) and duration of assistance (e.g., hours per day).

Another study evaluated the effects of an occupational therapy intervention program involving home visits targeted at helping caregivers modify the home environment to address daily caregiving demands; the findings indicated that the interventions had a "modest effect on dementia patients' IADL dependence" (Gitlin, Corcoran, Winter, Boyce, & Hauck, 2001, p. 4). This study also found that, among some subgroups of caregivers, "the program improves their self-efficacy and upset in specific areas of caregiving" (p. 4).

■ ■ ■

Occupational Therapy and Home Modifications

Occupational Therapy Process

The *home modification process* has been defined as the confluence of activities and delivery of services, including assessing needs, identifying solutions, implementing solutions, training in use of solutions, and evaluating outcomes (Sanford, 2004). Occupational therapy plays a significant role in assessing needs, identifying and training in solutions, and evaluating outcomes. The occupational therapy process consists of evaluation, intervention, and outcomes. Figure 3 depicts the relationship of the occupational therapy process to the home modification process.

In some practices, aspects of the process of occupational therapy are reported using Current Procedural Terminology (CPT)™ codes (see Appendix C). The following section describes the occupational therapy process as it relates to the home modification process.

Referral

The need for occupational therapy may be identified at various points in the home modification process. In some instances, particularly in traditional health care settings, a client is referred for occupational therapy, and the practitioner identifies the need for home modifications in addition to other occupational therapy interventions. In other cases, an occupational therapist is contacted specifically to assess the need for home modifications, to identify home modification solutions, or to train the client to use the modifications to optimize performance and participation.

Emergence of the need for home modifications may or may not coincide with the onset of a change in client factors (e.g., body structure or function). A sudden, traumatic change (e.g., amputation, spinal cord injury, stroke) will likely result in an altered interaction with the environment. Chronic conditions may exacerbate (e.g., arthritis, multiple sclerosis, Parkinson's disease), or there may be a gradual decline (e.g., in vision, balance,

Occupational Therapy Process	Home Modification Process
Evaluation	Assessing needs
Intervention	
Planning	Identifying solutions
Implementation	Training in solutions
Review	Assessing needs/Evaluating outcomes
Outcomes	Evaluating outcomes

Figure 3. Relationship of occupational therapy process to home modification process.

dexterity) that results in an increasingly unsatisfactory interaction with the environment and, thus, unsatisfactory performance. There also are circumstances in which there is no change in body structure or function, but a change in physical or social context occurs, altering the fit between activity demands and performance skills and performance patterns. This results in ineffective or disrupted performance of occupations. Changes in physical or social context may include a move to a new home or a change in the ability or availability of a caregiver who has assisted with performance of activities in the home. For example, a client with limited mobility and endurance depends on a spouse to assist with personal care and home management. The spouse develops back pain, which limits physical activity. The couple now needs modifications to enhance the participation of the spouse needing assistance and to reduce the physical demands on the spouse offering assistance. Acquisition of a new role may involve new tasks with activity demands that exceed the performance skills of the individual. For example, a client who uses a wheelchair has a baby. The new child care tasks require modifications to the environment to enable safe, satisfactory management of the infant's needs by the parent using the wheelchair.

Often an individual simply experiences problems performing necessary or desired activities. The underlying causes of the problem may not be recognized as related to the environment and in fact may be attributed to personal inadequacy. As a result, individuals often respond to these problems by curtailing their activities, seeking assistance from others, or depending on others to perform activities. These individuals are unaware that there may be options to modify the home to restore a person–environment fit. For example, an older person feels unsafe stepping into and out of the bathtub to take a shower and so decides to discontinue showering and instead perform sponge bathing.

In some cases, the need for home modifications may be identified before involvement of occupational therapy, but determination of the most appropriate modifications requires the referral to an occupational therapist. This may occur in situations in which an individual recognizes that the environment is contributing to unsatisfactory or unsafe occupational performance but lacks adequate knowledge to identify the appropriate modification. The individual may query a medical equipment vendor regarding types of bath seats available or seek advice from hardware store or home center staff regarding grab bar placement or ramp slope. The individual may identify a contractor or other individual to install modifications but still lack assurance that the changes will be appropriate or adequate. In these cases, the person may be referred to an occupational therapist to further evaluate his or her needs and refine the proposed solutions to ensure that modifications meet those needs.

Evaluation

The occupational therapy evaluation consists of two components: (1) development of the occupational profile and (2) analysis of occupational performance. The occupational therapist elicits information from the client about needs, problems, risks, and concerns. The occupational profile includes the client's occupational history, patterns of living, interests, values and needs, and priorities. The occupational therapist may select specific assessment tools or procedures to assess performance patterns and performance skills. In evaluating, the occupational therapist considers stability or instability of performance patterns and performance skills and client factors.

The occupational therapist also seeks to understand personal factors (WHO, 2001), including the meaning the home has to the client, the relationship of the home to the client's sense of self and sense of place, and the expectations the client has of his or her own performance. Rather than simply assessing a physical space or observing isolated performance, the occupational therapist will seek to understand the meaning of home and the daily routines and rituals that are part of that meaning. "Everyone relates to form, spaces, objects, memories, and messages—the elements that collectively comprise the creation called *home*—in different ways" (Bachner, 2000, p. 19). The word *performance* alludes to an actor on a stage before an audience, with props used effectively to convey a message to an audience. Similarly, the home and its contents provide props and a stage for a client to express his or her identity to visitors (Goffman, 1959). It is essential to appreciate the identity the client wishes to convey to appreciate the meaning and utility of the "props" that make up the home. The meaning of "home" must be respected and maintained as modifications occur, yet it can be easily overlooked and disrupted if not identified before the implementation of any modification. The meaning of home and the meaning of occupations performed in the home are greatly influenced by the client's spiritual, social, temporal, and cultural contexts. The occupational therapist seeks to understand these meanings during the evaluation as they influence the nature, feasibility, and appropriateness of interventions.

When home modifications are being considered, the occupational therapy evaluation occurs in the home. In cases in which the client is receiving occupational therapy services in a health care setting, the development of the occupational profile and some aspects of analysis may be conducted in that setting.

However, for the occupational therapist to accurately assess activity demands and features of the environment, the evaluation should include a visit to the home with the client present to evaluate person–environment interaction in context.

The occupational therapist analyzes the physical environment of the home as it enhances or constrains performance. Lawton (1980) classified environments based on the demands they place on the client. He termed this construct *environmental press* and hypothesized that the interaction of a person's abilities and the demands of the environment shaped performance. In this paradigm, clients with high levels of competence can tolerate a wider range of environmental press with a greater likelihood of effective performance. Clients with lower levels of competence require a more limited range of environmental press to achieve effective performance.

Occupational therapy practitioners use the term *activity demands* to incorporate the concept of environmental press (e.g., space demands, objects required and their properties) as well as the social demands, temporal demands, required actions, and required underlying body functions and structures needed to carry out an activity. Because the physical space and the tools available in the home differ from those available in a health care setting, a client's performance may be effective when evaluated in the care setting but ineffective or unsafe in the home setting. By conducting the evaluation in the home, the occupational therapist can assess activity demands accurately and determine the "fit" between activity demands and client capacities.

Intervention

After obtaining the occupational profile and analyzing occupational performance, intervention plans and goals are established in collaboration with the client, the family, and other members of the team. Goals must reflect the client's potential to benefit from home modifications, specific contextual factors (e.g., personal, social, and cultural contexts; financial resources), adaptability of the home environment (e.g., structural integrity), right to modify (e.g., ownership or permis-

sion granted by the owner or owners), and areas of occupation most important to the client and family members.

The client's definitions of independence, safety, and autonomy guide the process of identifying desired outcomes. For one person, letting a spouse complete a specific task allows the time and energy to perform a more enjoyable task; for another, the completion of the task, no matter how difficult or time-consuming, provides ultimate satisfaction. Although "safety" is often regarded as the presence or absence of hazardous features, most home environments are not inherently safe or unsafe. Reduction of risk associated with an activity may be identified as an important outcome. In cases in which a caregiver is expected to be involved in the activity, reduction of risk to both client and caregiver may be a desired outcome.

The basis for all occupational therapy intervention in the environment is the person–environment fit as it relates to occupational engagement. Interventions are identified and prioritized based on their relevance to the occupations important to the client. An occupational therapist will use the occupations of the client as the point of reference for identifying interventions and determining targeted outcomes that may be achieved through home modifications. This is in contrast to a room-by-room audit, followed by modifications based on standards or guidelines, a common approach recommended for public facilities (e.g., to retrofit the facility for compliance with the Americans With Disabilities Act [ADA], P.L. 101-336). These audit approaches do not consider the abilities or preferences of the user nor of the activities to be performed but instead focus solely on aspects of the physical environment, usually as a basis for specific modifications to improve access or reduce risk.

Intervention Approaches and Strategies

Education and Consultation

In circumstances in which a client, family member, or care manager is considering home modifications, education is often the first need to be addressed. For many people, home modification is a new concept or is associated only with features seen in public facilities, such as the steel grab bars installed in accessible toilet stalls in public bathrooms. If a client perceives home modification as change that will make the home seem "institutional" or unusual, the client may have misgivings. In some cases, the client may be open to the prospect, but a family member sharing the home is resistant to the idea. In many situations, a client or family may be so focused on the client's impairments or limited skills that they have not considered how the environment may be adapted to optimize the client's abilities.

When a third-party funding source is involved, that funding source may need to be educated regarding the outcomes to be achieved through home modifications. Many third-party insurers categorize interventions directed toward remediating impairments as "medically necessary" but categorize interventions directed toward the environment as "personal convenience." In most cases, this categorization is not negotiable. However, some funding sources may be persuaded that, for a given client, anticipated outcomes of home modification, including reduction in need for assistance and reduction in risk during activities, justify allocation of funding for home modifications.

In all situations, the occupational therapist will evaluate for the need and the appropriateness of home modifications and identify how the proposed modifications will change the need for assistance (caregiving) required by the client. The occupational therapist or occupational therapy assistant also can help the client, the family, and the payer analyze the benefits in terms of saving caregiver time and cost and reducing the risk of injury to client and caregiver. In some instances, benefits also may be analyzed in terms of keeping a client in the home (preventing institutional placement) and enabling the client to participate in educational activities or employment (in or outside the home) or enabling a caregiver either to return to work outside the home or to increase work hours outside the home. This analysis may include prioritizing the modifications, which is necessary when modification needs exceed the resources available to fund them or when the implementation of modifications is expected to

occur over time. The practitioner also may provide resources, such as photographs, catalogs, and videotapes, that demonstrate the appearance or use of the proposed modification as it will be when installed. This helps communicate the purpose and use to a client or a family member, as well as to ease concerns about "institutional" appearances.

In some situations, all that is expected from the occupational therapist is consultation. This may be what the payer or the client wants, or it may be all that it needed. For example, a life care planner requests an occupational therapy consultation to identify home modification needs and projected outcomes for a client involved in an injury or liability action. The occupational therapy consultation yields recommendations to incorporate in the proposed life care plan. In other situations, the modifications needed are commercially available or incorporate principles of universal design (Center for Universal Design, 1997b) that enable the user to use the modification safely and effectively with little or no further training or follow-up from occupational therapy (see Appendix B).

Education and Training

When modifications have more complexity, or there are barriers to learning, the occupational therapist or occupational therapy assistant may provide training in the use of the modifications after they have been installed. In some situations, modifications may have already been installed before referral to occupational therapy, but difficulties using the modifications prompt the client to seek an occupational therapist.

Many daily occupations are performed habitually in a specific manner. Training may be needed to effectively incorporate modifications into activity routines that become habitual. For example, a client with weakness or impaired balance has always taken tub baths but seeks the advice of an occupational therapist for modifications to bathe safely and reduce the risk of falling. The client is aware of the variety of bath seats but finds the prospect of not being able to move out of the shower spray undesirable. Based on the occupational therapist's recommendation, the client obtains a specific type of bath seat and handheld shower. The occupational therapy assistant trains the client in a specific technique to access the seat, eliminating the need to step over the tubside. The occupational therapy assistant also establishes a sequence for arranging task materials and controlling the handheld shower so that all items are in reach during the shower and the water flow is contained behind the shower curtain. After "rehearsing" this sequence as a "dry run" and then taking several showers with someone nearby for reassurance, the client establishes a new bathing routine incorporating the modifications. Bathing is once again performed to the client's satisfaction, but with greater safety and less effort.

Training to incorporate modifications into occupations is most needed when the modifications are extensive or complex, when new routines must be established, when impairments are newly acquired or recently exacerbated, or when caregivers must learn how to operate or incorporate the modifications in the course of providing assistance. In some cases, even modifications that are based on the principles of universal design require training and practice to incorporate their use into habits and routines. These are situations in which the modifications represent a substantial change in comparison to the pre-modification environment or situations in which the client was unable to perform activities in the pre-modification environment, no relevant habits existed, and effective habits must be established.

Family and Caregiver Education

In situations in which modifications are implemented to reduce the need for or demands on a caregiver, the caregiver should be instructed regarding the introduction of the modifications so that assistance can be appropriately "phased out" or reduced as the client develops increased competence and confidence in using the modifications. In many instances, modifications reduce the need for assistance from "hands on" to "being available." In some situations, modifications may eliminate the need for assistance entirely.

In some circumstances, family members or caregivers also may need specific training regarding the integration and safe use of home modifications. When modifications are designed to meet the needs of a child or an adult with cognitive impairments, a family member or caregiver should be instructed in how to operate all modifications and devices and should understand all precautions and safety issues that may pertain. Training also may be appropriate regarding the care and maintenance of the device or modification. It is important that others who may be assisting the client or using the modifications be trained so that the modifications are used safely and effectively and not damaged or rendered ineffective. Caregivers may be parents, spouses, personal care attendants, or others who provide assistance to the client. Others who may need instruction in the use of modifications include other family members who live in the home and who also may use the modifications.

It may be difficult for a caregiver to recognize how modification of the physical environment may affect behaviors associated with severe conditions such as dementia. Caregivers may have developed habits of responding to behaviors by providing more care and attention. This may encourage the client to be more dependent and to seek more attention (Pynoos, Cohen, & Lucas, 1988). Caregivers may need education to understand how the modifications can reduce caregiver stress and burden as well as increase the safety and participation of the client (Calkins & Namazi, 1991; Corcoran & Gitlin, 1992; Gitlin et al., 2001). This education optimizes the effectiveness of the modifications for the client and caregivers.

Intervention Implementation

The following section describes home modification strategies that might be used to address problems with performing occupations, focusing specifically on occupations that are most commonly performed in the home. These problems arise from activity demands that are not compatible with a client's performance skills. The interventions described are offered to illustrate occupational therapy and home modification interventions to achieve a better fit between performance skills and activity demands, thus enhancing occupational performance. The section includes only a small sample

> **ADL Problem: Bathing and transferring for a client with mobility limitations**
>
> **Modifications:** Curbless shower stall, handheld shower, and grab bars
> **Training:** To incorporate use of modifications and establish bathing routine
> **Outcome:** The client no longer needs assistance and showers independently.

of occupations that may be addressed and interventions that may be identified.

Activities of Daily Living

Activities of daily living (ADLs) are activities performed to care for self. ADLs depend on complex interactions between the person and the environment. Unique features of ADLs are their familiarity and frequency. Because they are performed so often for so long (over the lifespan), they form *habits* and *routines* that are performed with little conscious effort or attention to their execution. However, a change in client factors and performance skills or in the physical context can disrupt or obstruct performance of ADLs.

Disrupted performance as the result of changes in body structure or function may be obvious. A client with a fractured wrist may have to learn new ways to eat, shave, comb hair, write, turn a key, or hold a telephone while the joint is immobilized in a cast. In this case, the disruption, like the impairment, is likely to be temporary. A client with paraplegia from a spinal cord injury must learn new ways to move about, dress, bathe, and toilet on a permanent basis. The use of a wheelchair for mobility will require significant changes in the home environment to allow the client to perform ADLs with altered abilities. Once home modifications are completed, new habits and routines must be developed to enable performance of activities previously taken for granted.

In the case of a profound, permanent change in the body, the home must be reconfigured to fit the client for effective new habits to develop. An occupational therapy evaluation will identify modifications that address both immediate and longer term needs for the environment to fit the wheelchair user while considering emotional response to injury, tolerance for change, potential health risks, and sequelae associated with the health condition. The extent of such an evaluation and of interventions depends on the priorities of the client and the resources available for modifications.

Some changes in body structure and function are less obvious but are equally profound in altering performance skills and disrupting habits and routines. Many chronic illnesses result in chronic low energy. Clients with low energy need more frequent rests, requiring routines to be divided into manageable segments of energy expenditure. Actions that take more energy, such as reaching, standing (as in a shower), or walking, may consume significant energy reserves and force the client to postpone or cancel activities if energy is depleted. For clients who experience chronic energy limitations, the environment can be modified to reduce activity demands (e.g., duration, effort). An occupational therapy practitioner can identify changes to the environment that present minimal disruptions to habits while reducing demands of effort and time.

> **ADL Problem: Morning personal care for a client with chronic low energy**
>
> **Modifications:** Storage of garments relocated in proximity to bathroom; seat installed in the bathroom for drying and dressing; grooming supplies relocated to the bathroom; and installation of shower seat, grab bar, and handheld shower
> **Training:** To incorporate use of modifications and establish modified routine
> **Outcome:** The client performs the morning routine in 45 minutes without fatigue.

Changes in the environment can be disruptive to habits and routine. This is commonly experienced when away from home and performing a morning routine in a different bedroom and bathroom. Even a simple task such as adjusting water temperature or pressure for a shower in an unfamiliar bath is evidence of how habits are situated in a familiar physical context. While the activity may be performed adequately and safely, it requires more effort and attention because the habitual performance has been disrupted by a change in the environment.

A client with impairments of body structure or function may sustain ADL habits that are effective and satisfying, but these habits may be disrupted by a change in the environment. For example, an older client experiences a gradual decline in vision over several years. Over time, the client makes minor adjustments in routines and activity demands to accommodate to the losses but continues to participate in ADLs satisfactorily. Then the client moves to a new apartment in a new neighborhood to be near adult children. The habits that were established and embedded in the old environment are incompatible with the new environment, and the person now experiences ADL limitations with risks to safety. In this case, occupational therapy intervention focuses on environmental features and devices compatible with impaired vision while seeking to adapt the environment to more closely match the previous ADL habits and routines. Intervention also includes direct training in the use of modifications to re-establish new habits and to determine their efficacy and safety.

Some changes in body function are progressive and profound and result in global impairments. The most common of these is senile dementia of the Alzheimer's type. While the disease initially affects cognitive function, as it progresses it affects mood and behavior, and in later stages it affects motor function. A home modification evaluation for a client with dementia includes the cognitive, behavioral, and motor function of the client and the needs and abilities of the caregiver as well as the features of the physical environment. If the evaluation is conducted in the early stages of the condition, home modifications may be directed toward maintaining the ability to participate in ADLs. As the disease progresses, a subsequent evaluation may be needed with modifications that enable the client to participate in the activity while preventing behavioral problems and reducing physical demands on the caregiver. In later stages of the disease, home modifications may be implemented to reduce risk, achieve adequate hygiene, and maintain stimulation at a level the client can tolerate while limiting physical burden and emotional upset of the caregiver.

> **IADL Problem: A client with profound mobility limitations cannot extinguish the lights or secure the home after caregivers leave; caregivers cannot access the home unless the client provides them with keys**
>
> **Modifications:** Installation of EADL at bedside, which locks and unlocks doors and operates lights remotely; installation of intercom for caregivers (or other visitors) to communicate with client from outside the home
>
> **Outcome:** The client can secure the home and control access to the home without distributing keys or leaving the doors unlocked.

Instrumental Activities of Daily Living

Instrumental activities of daily living (IADLs) include the care of others and pets, child rearing, communication device use, community mobility, financial management, health management and maintenance, home establishment and maintenance, meal preparation and cleanup, safety procedures and emergency responses, and shopping. Although some of these activities are performed as routinely as ADLs, others are performed infrequently and may occur only in a specialized area of the home or the community and may require specific tools or equipment.

Meal preparation activities involve the use of tools and appliances that may present significant risk if they are misused. Retrieving, carrying, opening containers, cutting, chopping, measuring, mixing, operating appliance controls, following recipes, timing preparation and cooking procedures, and washing utensils are some of the performance skills that make up meal preparation. Performance of these skills can be affected by changes in client factors such as strength, endurance, mobility, balance, dexterity, vision, tactile sensation, and cognition. Occupational therapy interventions may include modifications to compensate for changes in client factors to perform these tasks effectively and safely. In some cases, the interventions may focus on performance of simplified occupations, such as modifications to

enable cold meal preparation and heating meals in a microwave oven. This might be an appropriate intervention if the occupational therapist determines that more complex meal preparation is not feasible or poses excessive risk (e.g., client has cognitive impairments and cannot perform simultaneous task steps or operate stove or conventional oven safely but cannot arrange assistance or meal delivery for all meals).

Changes in sensory function are less obvious but also can be disruptive to IADL performance and safety. For example, a client with impaired hearing may be reluctant to use the telephone because sounds are muffled, making conversation difficult. This same client may be unable to hear the sound of the doorbell or telephone ringing or the warning of a smoke alarm. There are adaptations available for all of these devices to optimize sound or to augment sound with a signal perceptible through other senses (e.g., strobe light, vibratory alert). When considering modifications to compensate for a sensory impairment, an occupational therapist assesses the client's tolerance for change and for "gadgets," the stability or anticipated progression of the sensory impairment, and the presence or absence of other impairments.

Control of the environment, including ventilation, illumination, and access, is an often-overlooked aspect of IADLs. Standard home construction practices for

> **IADL Problem: Meal preparation for a client with low vision**
>
> **Modifications:** Application of high-contrast and tactile cues on controls on microwave oven and stove; installation of task lighting in meal preparation area; resurfacing of work areas to increase contrast and reduce glare
>
> **Training:** Training to use new devices and strategies that rely on tactile and auditory input to establish new habits and incorporate them into existing meal preparation routines
>
> **Outcome:** The client can prepare simple and moderately complex meals safely without assistance.

IADL Problem: Caregiver with chronic back pain cares for a spouse with moderate dementia, experiencing increased pain and difficulty while assisting spouse with bathing

Modifications: Bathroom renovation with wet area, wall-mounted pull-down bath seat and handheld shower, 36-inch doorway

Training: Instruct in use of modifications; instruct caregiver in providing simple, one-step cues to direct the spouse through the bathing routine to wash and dry self while caregiver monitors safety and adequacy of bathing and drying

Outcome: Physical burden on the caregiver is minimized (setting water temperature and pressure and, if necessary, controlling the hand shower) while hygiene adequacy is maintained. Caregiving spouse also has an accessible shower to perform his or her own personal care.

Long-Term Outcomes: If the dementia progresses to a point when the spouse with dementia can no longer walk safely in the wet area, the caregiving spouse can use a wheeled bath seat to roll the spouse into and out of the bathroom and wet area without the risk of having the care recipient standing or walking in the wet area.

IADL Problem: Managing infant care for a client who uses a wheelchair

Modifications: Crib, changing table, and storage installed or modified to height accessible from wheelchair

Outcome: The client performs infant care from the wheelchair independently.

location of light switches, electrical outlets, thermostats, and fan controls often result in placements that are difficult to access or problematic for clients with limited mobility, dexterity, or vision or for those who are significantly taller or shorter than the "average" adult. Opening, closing, and locking windows present similar challenges. Limitations in dexterity, mobility, and strength also may restrict a client's ability to control access to the home or to exit the home quickly using standard door knobs, locks, and keys. Inability to control the environment may result in isolation, vulnerability to crime, injuries or illness from exposure to temperature extremes, and injuries from fall hazards not detected owing to poor illumination.

Newer technologies have produced electronic aids to daily living (EADLs), which enable a client to control any or all of these features of the environment with reduced demands for dexterity, mobility, and vision. Some EADLs also can operate a telephone remotely and may allow the user to control ventilation, illumination, and access (door locks) throughout the house from the bedside or a favorite chair. Remote controls also are available to operate a range of appliances as well as combination TV/VCR/DVD/cable remote controls. Some EADLs do not require dexterity; others do not require intact vision. An occupational therapy evaluation includes identification of EADLs that fit the client's needs and abilities, including the client's tolerance for technology and for complexity as well as consideration of possible progression of a disability and the compatibility of a given EADL system with expected future performance skills.

Often care of others is overlooked as a reason for home modifications. It may be assumed that caregiving, whether assisting another person to perform a task or doing a task for another person, is the only solution to the care recipient's needs. In some situations, caregiving may be perceived as less expensive than modifications to the environment that might make caregiving unnecessary or might reduce the burden. For example, helping an older spouse shower might be considered less burdensome and costly than remodeling the bathroom to remove a tub and installing a curbless shower or wet area. However, this strategy depends on the willingness and ability of the caregiving spouse to transfer the client into and out of the tub and to wash and rinse the client safely and adequately. Aside from the time commitment required by the caregiving spouse, this strategy also demands significant motor skills to assist the client safely and prevent injury to both people. These demands may not be considered until the caregiving spouse experiences a decline in motor skills or an incident such as a fall occurs, which then places the effectiveness of the entire strategy into question. In many instances, the result is that the care-receiving spouse is no longer showered but instead receives a sponge bath from either the caregiving spouse or from another caregiver (recruited from or hired by the family). Seldom is the time commitment, physical ability, or risk actually compared to the potential benefits of the accessible shower and the possibility that, with such a shower, the care recipient might be able to participate in bathing or even bathe himself or herself.

This caregiving dilemma also occurs when the care recipient is a child. Often caregiving habits that were formed when the child was younger, smaller, and more compliant with parental direction become less effective or more risky as the child grows, weighs more, or is interested in exploring the environment and testing parental limits. For example, a small child with cerebral palsy may be bathed in a bathtub by a parent. This strategy, which requires bending over the tub, is uncomfortable for the caregiver but effective. However, as the child grows, the risk and effort involved in lifting the child in and out of the tub increases. As the child's interest in the environment increases with age, splashing and squirming may increase, resulting in the parent getting wet. If the child has limited ability to sit unsupported, the parent also must provide support as well as assistance with washing. When the effort or the risk becomes too great, the parents may simply alter strategies and sponge bathe the child in bed. An occupational therapy evaluation can identify appropriate bathroom modifications to allow safer bathing, reducing demands for lifting and transferring and, if desired, allowing the child to bathe himself or herself.

Caregiving activities also are a focus of occupational therapy evaluation and intervention when a parent experiences a disability that affects child care activities. In these cases, the occupational therapist must balance the need for child safety with the parent's need for accessibility. This should be an ongoing discussion between occupational therapist and client whenever improved access for a client may potentially compromise the safety of a toddler or child living in or visiting the home.

Education and Work

Home modifications also may enable a client to obtain employment within or outside the home. This relationship of home modifications and "employ-ability" is often the justification for involvement of vocational rehabilitation services in the home modification process. The ability to manage care of self and basic care of the home is a necessary prerequisite for sustaining employment outside the home. With recent advances in technology, employed work from the home is also more common and may be more feasible for many clients. In these cases, home modifications to create or adapt a work area in the home may enable employment for a client who might otherwise be unable to access work environments away from the home.

Education and work-related activities in the home may be conducted in a home office or in a child's study area. Occupational therapy evaluation may include specific activity demands of educational or work occupations. Interventions may include environmental supports to increase access, reduce fatigue, or enable the client to focus on the task without distractions.

Education Problem: Client is in elementary school, uses a wheelchair, and must complete homework assignments using the computer

Modifications: Computer workstation modified for wheelchair access; installation of accessible bookshelves and storage for educational supplies

Training: Instruction to parents to terminate previous routines (retrieving materials for child, transcribing assignments) to facilitate child's autonomy

Outcome: The client completes homework assignments without parental assistance.

> **Leisure Problem: A client with low vision is unable to operate television or audio/stereo system using on-device controls or supplied remote controls**
>
> **Modification:** EADL with tactile and oversized buttons to control television and audio system
>
> **Training:** Instruction in use of device; provision of large-print instructions with enlarged graphic of the EADL controls
>
> **Outcome:** The client operates the audio system and television, selecting stations, CDs, and channels independently.

Play and Leisure

Play and leisure in and about the home encompasses a variety of activities occurring indoors and outdoors. Outdoor home modifications may be considered in relation to accessibility of the home but are seldom considered in relation to play and leisure. Most outdoor play equipment for children is not designed for parents or children with limited mobility. An occupational therapist can evaluate and identify equipment or

> **Leisure Problem: A client recently began using a motorized wheelchair for all mobility. An outdoor lift has been installed to permit access to and from house, but the client has been an avid gardener and cannot access the flower beds**
>
> **Modifications:** Installation of raised planting beds installed with 3-side access and level approach; grading of pathways to allow power wheelchair access to selected ground-level flower beds
>
> **Training:** Instruction to operate wheelchair on outdoor pathways; incorporation of gardening tools to weed and prune ground-level plants; training to position the wheelchair for optimal access to raised beds
>
> **Outcome:** The client continues to engage in gardening.

modifications that enable both the parents and the children to engage in play. Gardening is a common outdoor leisure pursuit that many adults are forced to abandon when they experience impairments in mobility, strength, or balance. An occupational therapy evaluation identifies modification solutions to enable a client to continue with gardening activities.

Within the home, entertainment equipment such as televisions, videocassette recorders, audio systems, computerized games, and video recording equipment have complicated controls typically requiring acute vision and fine dexterity to operate effectively. An occupational therapist evaluates the client's "gadget tolerance" as well as the client's skills and abilities and the devices the client wishes to operate to identify appropriate EADLs. Intervention may include training in use of the EADL as well as appropriate placement of equipment to increase access. Within the home, play areas for children or hobby areas for adults can be designed around the desires and interests of the client and the family.

Other Professionals Involved in Home Modification Implementation

The process of planning, designing, and constructing home modifications most often involves a team of individuals with complementary expertise. This team may include an occupational therapist, design and construction professionals, and case managers or representatives of payers or community organizations. The role of the occupational therapist on the team is defined by the services offered by the practitioner, the extent of the modifications, the skill mix of the other team members, and the scope of occupational therapy practice as it is defined in the state or jurisdiction where services are being provided. Some of the other team members involved in the home modification process are described as follows.

Architects and Interior Designers

An architect may develop and refine the design, prepare the construction documents, and coordinate with the contractor on projects that involve significant structural changes to the home. Professional interior designers specialize in designing effective, aesthetically pleasing modifications or reconfigurations of the home environment. Involvement of an interior designer is especially valuable when modifications are extensive, as in situations where more than one room is modified or when more than one configuration of the environment is feasible. In some jurisdictions, interior designers also may execute the role of general contractor for home modifications that are less extensive or cost less than a specified dollar amount.

Contractors, Remodelers, and Tradespeople

For most projects, a contractor may develop the design with input from the occupational therapist, the client and, where appropriate, the interior designer. The general contractor is responsible for securing building permits, adhering to local codes and regulations, securing inspections, and directing the work of subcontractors. Because many contractors are more familiar with accessibility issues in commercial and institutional construction, the occupational therapist may have a role in translating "accessibility" to the home environment. For example, most contractors are familiar with grab bars designed for commercial and institutional applications but may not be familiar with grab bars designed for residential applications. The occupational therapist or occupational therapy assistant may be a resource for directing the contractor to appropriate sources for such devices.

Since the passage of the ADA in 1990, some contractors have mistakenly assumed that the standards for accessibility developed for the ADA apply to residential construction. The ADA does not apply to private homes. However, local building codes apply to structural modifications, and the local building inspector should be consulted if any questions arise as to whether a proposed custom modification meets local codes.

Home modifications involving building, carpentry, plumbing, electrical, or ventilation may involve subcontractors or tradespeople in these specialties. The number of subcontractors involved will depend on the extent and complexity of the modifications. These

services are secured by and are under the direction of the general contractor.

In cases in which modifications involve little or no structural change, an individual with experience in carpentry and home repair may be hired by the homeowner to build or install modifications. Although most of these projects do not require permits, the homeowner is responsible for determining whether a permit is needed (e.g., for a ramp) and securing such a permit before the worker proceeds. Such service providers may or may not be regulated by local authorities, and it is wise for the homeowner to obtain references and determine the specific expertise of the worker as well as whether the worker has liability insurance or is bonded. Examples of modifications appropriate for such a worker may include installation of grab bars, construction of new cupboards or shelves for accessible storage, installation of replacement lighting fixtures, installation of stair railings, construction of a simple ramp, and other simple projects. In all these cases, the occupational therapist coordinates with the client and the worker to ensure that modifications are executed appropriately to match the client's skills, preferences, and needs.

Volunteers and "Do-It-Yourselfers"

When a home modification is under the auspices of a community organization, such as Rebuilding Together, or a community action agency, volunteers may make up all or most of the workforce for the project. The technical skills and knowledge of these volunteers may vary, but the coordinating organization is responsible for involving individuals with adequate expertise to supervise the volunteers and ensure a safe, adequate result that complies with local codes.

Some home modifications will be completed by "do-it-yourselfers" who are friends or family of the client. Many simple modifications can be made by a do-it-yourselfer with basic carpentry skills and knowledge of residential electrical wiring. Simple plumbing, storage, lighting, and telephone modifications may be managed by a layperson instructed by the occupational therapist as to the specific devices and materials needed for the modification. These modifications may include installation of a handheld shower, installation of adapted telephones, installation of simple EADLs, installation of task lights under a kitchen cupboard to illuminate a work area, or changing fixtures or intensity of lighting to directly illuminate reading areas or reduce glare, and other simple tasks. The occupational therapy practitioner coordinates with the client and the organization to ensure that modifications are executed appropriately to match the client's skills, preferences, and needs (Toto, 2001).

Intervention Review

The course of occupational therapy services involving home medications depends on the evaluation findings and the interventions agreed to. If the client seeks education and recommendations (consultation) only, services may be limited to providing recommendations that the client may then choose to act on as desired. If training is sought in addition to education, services extend through the installation of the modifications, and completion of services is identified when the client or caregiver goals are met. In most cases, this is when the client or caregiver is able to use the modifications satisfactorily during routine activities. If at any time the client does not desire to continue occupational therapy, the services are concluded.

Outcomes

The outcomes achieved through home modifications and occupational therapy vary in scope and magnitude. If a client has sought extensive modifications to address significant environmental "mis-fits," the outcomes may include enhancements in performance, satisfaction, and safety in a range of occupations and activities. Such broad outcomes are exemplified in the case of a client who seeks extensive modifications after sustaining an injury resulting in paraplegia and use of a wheelchair. The client's priorities are (1) being able to stay in her own home rather than move, (2) eliminating the need for a personal care attendant, (3) being able to prepare her own meals and do her own laundry, and (4) continuing two important and related leisure

occupations: gourmet cooking and growing herbs. The occupational therapy evaluation results in identification of extensive modifications, including construction of a wheelchair access entrance to the home, construction of a ground-floor-level bedroom and bathroom suite with wheelchair-accessible storage and fixtures, modifications to the kitchen for storage and appliance access with an adjoining laundry area, installation of EADLs for remote control of ventilation and illumination, and construction of raised gardening beds around the patio. After implementation of the modifications, follow-up training with the occupational therapist and occupational therapy assistant addresses many specific tasks to adapt the client's prior habits and routines and incorporate the new modifications to achieve the outcomes defined by the client's priorities.

Other outcomes are narrower in scope. For example, a client with Parkinson's disease has been receiving bathing assistance from his spouse, but this burden has become too great. The client wants to continue showers, but both the client and the spouse are concerned about the cost of hiring a home care aide, and the client is anxious about having a "stranger" perform such intimate care. On the basis of these needs and priorities, the occupational therapist identifies appropriate bathroom modifications that fit the current and expected skills of the client and the caregiver. Once the modifications are installed, the occupational therapist trains both the client and spouse to use the modifications effectively and to incorporate the new devices into the evening bathing routine they both prefer. For the client, the primary outcome is being able to continue showering. For the client and the spouse, other outcomes include (1) reduced effort and risk associated with the client's bathing and (2) modifications that cost less than would six visits from a home care aide.

Follow-up Services

Because the need for home modifications may arise from changes in body structure and function, environment, physical or social context, or personal factors, the need for follow-up depends on whether subsequent changes in any of these areas result in a loss of occupational performance or an ineffective or unsatisfactory person–environment fit. A client with significant impairments of body structure and function may need home modifications each time there is a move to a new home. Re-initiation of an occupational therapy evaluation in the home may be required to further modify a home or to address changes in a new home.

■ ■ ■

Appendix A.
Glossary of Terms and Definitions, Homes for Life Coalition of Howard County, Maryland

Note. Italicized terms in definitions are defined elsewhere in this glossary.

Accessibility equipment

Devices that are used primarily by people with disabilities to provide access and exit, for example, a *ramp,* door opener, *elevator,* and stair lift.

Accessible

Describes an environment (e.g., home, building, facility) or portion thereof that is readily usable by people with different needs and abilities.

Accessible design

A dwelling that meets prescribed requirements for *accessible* housing. Mandatory requirements for accessible housing vary widely and are found in state, local, and model building codes; in agency regulations such as in the U.S. Department of Housing and Urban Development's Program 202 and 811, Section 504, and the Fair Housing Amendments Act of 1988 requirements. They also are found in standards such as the American National Standards Institute's A117.1 and the Uniform Federal Accessibility Standards.

Note. Adapted from Homes for Life Coalition of Howard County, Maryland. (2003). *Homes for life: Using universal design to create barrier-free homes for better living.* Ellicott City, MD: Author. For more information, contact Homes for Life Coalition of Howard County, Maryland, P.O. Box 6686, Ellicott City, MD 21042; 410-313-6410; www.hflc.org.

Accessible element/feature

Designs or products that, when placed in homes, make operation, access, or manipulation easier for all people. Most *accessible* features are determined by individual needs and are permanently fixed in place, for example, widened doorways, lowered countertop segments, switches and controls in easily reached locations, and pathways free of steps and stairs.

Accessible route

A continuous unobstructed pathway over which a person can travel, for example, a sidewalk.

Activities of daily living

Activities performed daily, including eating, grooming, bathing, dressing, transferring, and toileting.

ADAAG

Americans With Disabilities Act Accessibility Guidelines (see U.S. Access Board, 1994, n.d.).

Adaptability

The ability of certain building spaces and elements, such as kitchen counters, sinks, and grab bars, to be easily added or altered to accommodate the needs of individuals with or without disabilities or to accommodate the needs of people with different types or degrees of disability (U.S. Access Board, 1994, n.d.).

Adaptable home

A home that has design features that can be easily modified by removing barriers and adding accessible elements to meet an individual's requirements and changing needs. Standards for adaptable design have been incorporated into both American National Standards Institute and Uniform Federal Accessibility Standards. These standards specify adaptability criteria that provide a level of full accessibility when adjustments are made.

Aging in place

Enables people to live in their homes for as long as they are able (throughout their life span). Strategies to accomplish aging in place may include fall prevention, home repair and *home modifications,* access to mental health services, and services provided by caregivers. A wellness model that promotes the ability of people to live in their homes (however one defines home) and communities through different life stages.

Alteration

A change to a building that affects or could affect its usability. Alterations include, but are not limited to, remodeling, renovation, rehabilitation, reconstruction, historic restoration, resurfacing of circulation paths or vehicular ways, changes or rearrangement of the structural parts or elements, and changes or rearrangement in the plan configuration of walls and full-height partitions. Normal maintenance, reroofing, painting or wallpapering, or changes to mechanical and electrical systems are not alterations unless they affect the usability of the building (U.S. Access Board, 1994, n.d.).

Americans With Disabilities Act (ADA)

A major civil rights law, prohibiting discrimination on the basis of disability in the private and public sectors. It covers employment, public services, public accommodations, and telecommunications (U.S. Access Board, 1994, n.d.).

ANSI

An acronym used to refer to the American National Standards Institute A117.1-1998 standards for providing access and usability to buildings and facilities for people with physical disabilities.

Assistive device

Tools or products used by individuals who need assistance performing *activities of daily living,* for example, reachers, tongs, and knob-turners.

Assistive technology

Devices for personal use created specifically to enhance the physical, sensory, and cognitive abilities of people with disabilities and to help them function more independently (Opening Doors, 2000).

Barrier free

Rooms, entrances, and environments that are designed to minimize or eliminate barriers like steps; large steep grades or slopes; thresholds greater than 1/2"; and narrow, cluttered, or restrictive passages.

Circulation path

An exterior or interior way of passage from one place to another for pedestrians, including, but not limited to, walks, hallways, courtyards, stairways, and stair landings, for example, paths around kitchen counters, sofas, and beds (U.S. Access Board, 1994, n.d.).

Clear floor space

The minimum unobstructed floor or ground space required to accommodate a single, stationary wheelchair and occupant (U.S. Access Board, 1994, n.d.).

Clear open space

A term used to describe doorway or passageway opening width (this is not the door size). It is the distance from the edge of the opened door to the opposite side of the door frame.

Closed-circuit telephone

A telephone with dedicated line(s) that must be used to gain entrance to a building, for example, a house phone or intercom (U.S. Access Board, 1994, n.d.).

Common use

Refers to those interior and exterior rooms, spaces, or elements that are used by all residents, guests, and visitors (U.S. Access Board, 1994, n.d.).

Concrete Change

An organization dedicated to making all homes visitable by people with different abilities.

Curb cuts/ramp

A short ramp cutting through a curb or built up to it (U.S. Access Board, 1994, n.d.).

Detectable warning

A standardized feature to warn people with visual impairments of hazards on a circulation path, for example, textured yellow strips placed on curbs and *curb cuts* to alert people that the sidewalk is ending and audible signals to accompany the visual walk signal at intersections.

Dwelling unit

A single unit of residence for one or more people that provides a kitchen or food preparation area and spaces for living, bathing, sleeping, etc. (U.S. Access Board, 1994, n.d.).

Egress/exit

A continuous, unobstructed way of exit from any point in a building to a public way. A means of egress may comprise vertical and horizontal travel and may include intervening room spaces, doorways, hallways, corridors, passageways, balconies, *ramps,* stairs, enclosures, lobbies, horizontal exits, courts, and yards. An accessible means of egress is one that does not include stairs, steps, or escalators (U.S. Access Board, 1994, n.d.).

Element

An architectural or mechanical component of a building, facility, space, or site, for example, tele-

phone, *curb ramp,* door, drinking fountain, seating, or toilet (U.S. Access Board, 1994, n.d.).

Elevators

Devices used to raise or lower people or objects; they may be installed inside or outside dwellings.

Entrance/entry

Any point of access to a building or portion of a building or facility used for the purpose of people entering. An entrance includes the approach walk, the vertical access leading to the entrance platform, the entrance platform itself, vestibules if provided, the entry doors or gates, door thresholds, and the hardware of the entry doors or gates (U.S. Access Board, 1994, n.d.).

Equitable use

Home environments created to be accessible to users of different sizes and abilities.

Finished grade

Slope of the ground surface of a site after all construction, leveling, grading, and development has been completed.

Flexible use

Items that can be adapted to suit different needs and abilities.

Grab bars

A bar of wood or metal specifically designed to serve as a support usually found in the bathroom near the toilet and shower areas.

Ground floor

Any occupiable floor less than one story above or below grade with direct access to grade. A building or facility always has at least one ground floor and may have more than one ground floor as where a split-level entrance has been provided or where a building is built into a hillside (U.S. Access Board, 1994, n.d.).

Handheld shower

A shower head to which a hose has been attached allowing the user to take a shower from either a seated or standing position.

Handicap

Physical or mental impairment that substantially limits one or more major life activities.

Handrail

A bar of wood or metal specifically designed to serve as a support, usually found along a staircase or ramp.

Home modifications

Adaptations to living environments intended to increase usage, safety, security, and independence for the user. Home modifications are used in conjunction with assistive devices and home repairs.

Independent living movement

A civil rights movement holding that people with disabilities have the right to live self-directed lives in the community.

Independent living program

A community-based program that provides direct or indirect services necessary to help individuals with severe disabilities increase their self-determination and minimize dependence on others.

Lever handles

Fixtures that may be operated with flat hands, forearms, elbows, etc., to make opening doors, turning on water, etc., easier for people with limited grasp or strength.

Lifts

See *elevators*.

Low physical effort

The recommended amount of effort needed to operate or manipulate a device is less than 5 pounds of force.

Major life activities

Functions such as caring for one's self, performing manual tasks, walking, seeing, hearing, speaking, learning, breathing, and working (U.S. Department of Housing and Urban Development, 2000).

Marked crossing

A crosswalk or other identified path intended for pedestrian use in crossing a vehicular pathway (U.S. Access Board, 1994, n.d.).

Mezzanine or mezzanine floor

That portion of a story that is an intermediate floor level placed within the story and having occupiable space above and below its floor (U.S. Access Board, 1994, n.d.).

Multifamily dwelling

Any building containing more than two dwelling units (U.S. Access Board, 1994, n.d.).

Nonskid surface (slip resistant)

A slip-resistant surface to reduce slipping and falling when surface is wet. Specialized flooring or stripping can be added to bathtubs, shower floors, and exterior steps.

Operable part

A component part of equipment or an appliance that can be manipulated. An operable part may be used to insert or withdraw objects or to activate, deactivate, or adjust the equipment or appliance, for example, coin slots, push buttons, controls, and handles (U.S. Access Board, 1994, n.d.).

Pathway

Line of movement.

Perceptible information

Data that can be used and understood by people with different sensory abilities or that can be adapted to work with sensory devices.

Power-assisted door

A mechanism that helps to open doors, or relieves the opening resistance of a door, on the activation of a switch or a continued force applied to the door itself (U.S. Access Board, 1994, n.d.).

Public use

Describes interior or exterior rooms or spaces that are made available to the general public. Public use may be provided at a building or facility that is privately or publicly owned (U.S. Access Board, 1994, n.d.).

Raised toilet seat

Portable seat that fits over existing toilet seat to reduce the amount of knee and hip flexion involved when sitting on a toilet.

Ramp

A walking surface that is used to transverse an elevation change along a path. The maximum allowable slope for ramps is 1" rise for 12" of horizontal run.

Rehabilitation engineering

The science and study of applying scientific principles and engineering methodologies to address the mobility, communication, and transportation needs of people with disabilities (Opening Doors, 2000).

RESNA

Acronym for Rehabilitation Engineering and Technical Assistance Society of North America, an interdisciplinary association of people with a common interest in technology and disabilities that provides technical assistance in areas related to universal design and assistive technology.

Sensory accommodations

Accessible features or devices used to assist people with limited vision, limited hearing, or other sensory limitations. Sensory accommodations for people with visual limitations may include Braille and large-print signage, increased lighting, contrasting colors on walls or floors, and substitutions of auditory cues and messages for visual cues. Sensory accommodations for people with hearing impairments may include amplification and volume controls on telephones, text messages, and strobe or flashing lights on fire alarms and doorbells.

Shall

Denotes a mandatory specification or requirement (U.S. Access Board, 1994, n.d.).

Should

Denotes an advisory specification or recommendation (U.S. Access Board, 1994, n.d.).

Signage

Displayed verbal, symbolic, tactile, and pictorial information (U.S. Access Board, 1994, n.d.).

Simple and intuitive use

The use of the space and or feature is obvious and does not require instruction.

Site

A parcel of land bounded by a property line or a designated portion of a public right-of-way (U.S. Access Board, 1994, n.d.).

Site improvement

Landscaping, paving for pedestrian and vehicular ways, outdoor lighting, recreational facilities, and the like, added to a site (U.S. Access Board, 1994, n.d.).

Slope

The relative steepness of the land between two points. Slope can be determined by dividing the difference in elevation between two points by the distance between those points.

Cross slope: The slope that is perpendicular to the direction of travel. *Running slope:* The slope that is parallel to the direction of travel.

Space

A definable area, for example, room, toilet room, hall, assembly area, entrance, storage room, alcove, courtyard, or lobby (U.S. Access Board, 1994, n.d.).

Text telephone (TTY)

Machinery or equipment that uses interactive text-based communications through the transmission of coded signals across the standard telephone network. Text telephones can include, for example, devices known as TDDs (telecommunication display devices or telecommunication devices for deaf persons) or computers with special modems (U.S. Access Board, 1994, n.d.).

Tub seat/bench

Fixed or portable stool, bench, or seat that allows the individual to take a seated shower or bath. Seat height is usually adjustable.

Turning radius

The space needed for turning a wheelchair or electric scooter or other powered mobility devices. The *ADA* Architectural Guidelines recommend 60" (U.S. Access Code, 1994, n.d.).

Uniform Federal Accessibility Standards

A document that sets standards for facility accessibility by people with physical disabilities for federal and federally funded facilities (U.S. Access Board, 1994, n.d.).

Universal design

Design of products and environments to be usable by all people, to the greatest extent possible, without the need for adaptation or specialized design, for example, lowered light switches or levered doorknobs. Universal design benefits people of all ages and abilities. Universal design's Seven Principles are listed in Appendix B (Connell et al., 1997).

Vehicular way

A route intended for vehicular traffic, such as a street, driveway, or parking lot (U.S. Access Board, 1994, n.d.).

VISIT-Ability

An advocacy movement proposing that, when topographically feasible, basic access to all new homes is a civil right (RESNA, 703-524-6686).

Visitable home

A home that allows visitors and residents with different abilities and changing needs access to the main-floor living area. According to *Concrete Change,* visitable homes have one *zero-step entrance;* 32" clear passage through all interior doors, including bathrooms; and at least a half bath (preferably a full bath) on the main floor (Smith, 2000).

The Howard County Homes for Life Coalition adopted an expanded version of this definition in September 2001.

Walk

An exterior pathway with a prepared surface intended for pedestrian use (U.S. Access Board, 1994, n.d.).

Zero-step entrance

An entrance to a home or building that has a clear, unobstructed path or ramp and no more than a 1/2"-inch transition at the door's threshold.

References

Connell, B. R., Jones, M., Mace, R., Mueller, J., Mullick, A., Ostroff, E., et al. (1997). *The principles of universal design* (ver. 2.0). Raleigh: Center for Universal Design, North Carolina State University.

Opening Doors. (2000, June). Accessible housing for people with disabilities. *Opening Doors, 10.* Retrieved July 5, 2000, from http://www.c-c-d.org/od-june00. htm.

Smith, E. (2000). Construction guidelines for visitable homes. *Concrete Change.* Retrieved July 6, 2000, from http://www.concretechange.org/construc.htm.

U.S. Access Board. (1994). *Americans With Disabilities Act accessibility guidelines* (Appendix IV, 4201-10). Washington, DC: Thompson.

U.S. Access Board. (n.d.). *Americans With Disabilities Act accessibility guidelines for buildings and facilities.* Retrieved July 2000 from http://www.access-board.gov/adaag/html/adaag.htm.

U.S. Department of Housing and Urban Development. (2000). *Fair housing guidelines.* Retrieved July 11, 2000, from www.hud.gov/library/bookshelf09/fhefhag.cfm.

Bibliography

The committee used many resources to compile this glossary, including printed materials, the Internet, and personal experience. Where possible, original sources of terms are cited, but in most cases, the committee defined terms by synthesizing definitions from a variety of sources. The following Internet and printed resources were especially useful:

AARP. (1999). *Home safe home: How to prevent falls in the home.* Washington, DC: Author.

ABLEDATA. (1997, May). Fact sheet on ramps and accessible thresholds. *ABLEDATA Fact Sheet 27.* Retrieved from http://www.abledata.com.

ADA Information Center for the Mid-Atlantic Region at Trans Cen. (1999, Fall). *ADA in Focus, 3.3.*

American Occupational Therapy Association. (1998). Occupational therapy and adaptive equipment. *Developmental Disabilities Special Interest Section.*

American Occupational Therapy Association. (n.d.). Growing older in your home: Bathroom modifications for your changing needs. *News for You From the American Occupational Therapy Association* (Tip Sheet 6). Bethesda, MD: Author.

American Occupational Therapy Association. (n.d.). Growing older in your home: Bedroom modifications for your changing needs. *News for You From the American Occupational Therapy Association* (Tip Sheet 7). Bethesda, MD: Author.

American Occupational Therapy Association. (n.d.). Growing older in your home: Kitchen modifications for your changing needs. *News for You From the American Occupational Therapy Association* (Tip Sheet 24). Bethesda, MD: Author.

American Occupational Therapy Association. (n.d.). Home safety tips for the person with Alzheimer's disease. *News for You From the American Occupational Therapy Association* (Tip Sheet 24). Bethesda, MD: Author.

Christenson, M. A. (1999, November). Embracing universal design. *OT Practice*, pp. 12–15.

Connell, B. R., Jones, M., Mace, R., Mueller, J., Mullick, A., Ostroff, E., et al. (1997). *The principles of universal design* (ver. 2.0). Raleigh: Center for Universal Design, North Carolina State University.

Hare, P. (1992, Spring). Frail elders and the suburbs. *Generations, Journal of the American Society on Aging,* pp. 35–39.

HUD User. (1997, December). Report promotes home modification. *Recent Research Results.* Retrieved July 5, 2000, from http://www.huduser.org/periodicals/rrr.html.

Metropolitan Center for Independent Living. (n.d.). *How to build ramps for home accessibility.* Retrieved July 5, 2000, from www.MCIL-mn.org.

National Home of Your Own Alliance. (n.d.). *Position statement on home ownership and control.* Retrieved July 5, 2000, from http://alliance.unh.edu/aaposition.htm.

National Kitchen and Bath Association. (n.d.). *Adding interest and accessibility to your kitchen.* Retrieved July 5, 2000, from http://www.nkba.org.

National Kitchen and Bath Association. (n.d.). *Universal design: Plan kitchens that will last a lifetime.* Retrieved July 5, 2000, from http://www.nkba.org.

National Resource Center on Supportive Housing and Home Modification. (n.d.) *The toolbox.* Retrieved July 5, 2000, from http://www.homemods.org.

Opening Doors. (2000, June). Accessible housing for people with disabilities. *Opening Doors, 10.* Retrieved July 5, 2000, from http://www.c-c-d.org/od-june00. htm.

Ostroff, E. (2000). *Mining our natural resources: The user as expert.* Retrieved July 5, 2000, from http://www.adaptenv.org/index.php?option=Resource &articleid=150.

Pynos, J., et al. (1998). Improving the delivery of home modifications. *Technology and Disability, 8*(1–2), 3–14.

Salant, K. (1999, February 6). Going flat out. *The Washington Post,* p. G1.

Smith, E. (1990). Construction guidelines for visitable homes. *Concrete Change.* Retrieved July 6, 2000, from http://www.concretechange.org/construc.htm.

Truesdale, S., & Steinfield, E. (2002) *Visit-ability: An approach to universal design in housing.* Buffalo, NY: Rehabilitation Engineering Research Center on Universal Design.

Universal design: Homes for the future today. (1999). Irvine, CA: Irvine Company.

U.S. Access Board. (1994). *Americans With Disabilities Act accessibility guidelines* (Appendix IV, 4201-10). Washington, DC: Thompson.

U.S. Access Board. (n.d.). *Americans With Disabilities Act accessibility guidelines for buildings and facilities.* Retrieved July 2000 from http://www.access-board.gov/adaag/html/adaag.htm.

U.S. Architectural and Transportation Barriers Compliance Board. (1990, June). *UFAS accessibility checklist.* Washington, DC: Author.

U.S. Department of Housing and Urban Development. (2000). *Fair housing guidelines.* Retrieved July 11, 2000, from www.hud.gov/library/bookshelf09/fhefhag.cfm.

Wylde, M. A. (1996, April). Consumer knowledge of home modifications. *A blueprint for action: The Second National Working Conference on Home Modification Policy,* Washington, DC. Retrieved July 5, 2000, from http://www.homemods.org/library/pages/knowledge. html.

■ ■ ■

Appendix B.
Principles of Universal Design and Application to Home Modifications

The principles of universal design (see table below) convey some of the factors that occupational therapists consider when analyzing the demands of a client's activity. For example, occupational therapists consider space demands of an activity as well as tools used and their properties. As the occupational therapist considers the space within the home or the tools used, the therapist might use these principles to identify appropriate modifications. However, the therapist is most likely going to consider modifications and adaptations that are usable by the client, to the greatest extent possible, while maintaining usability for other inhabitants and considering future marketing and ownership of the dwelling.

In considering activity demands, occupational therapy practitioners also consider social demands and the social and cultural context. Acceptance and appropriateness is related to personal factors and to social and cultural contexts, factors that are related to, but may be more complex than, "marketability" cited in Principle 1. For example, a client may need zero-step access to the home. This can be accomplished through construction of a ramp or installation of an outdoor lift. Even if the costs and benefits are similar, the occupants may have different perceptions of what is appropriate and acceptable. A spouse may prefer the ramp because there is no mechanical or electric component that might require repair. A caregiver may prefer the lift

PRINCIPLES OF UNIVERSAL DESIGN

Principle	Definition of Principle
1. Equitable Use	The design is useful and marketable to people with diverse abilities.
2. Flexibility in Use	The design accommodates a wide range of individual preferences and abilities.
3. Simple and Intuitive Use	Use of the design is easy to understand, regardless of the user's experience, knowledge, language skills, or current concentration level.
4. Perceptible Information	The design communicates necessary information effectively to the user, regardless of ambient conditions or the user's sensory abilities.
5. Tolerance for Error	The design minimizes hazards and the adverse consequences of accidental or unintended actions.
6. Low Physical Effort	The design can be used efficiently and comfortably and with a minimum of fatigue.
7. Size and Space for Approach and Use	Appropriate size and space is provided for approach, reach, manipulation, and use regardless of user's body size, posture, or mobility.

because it eliminates pushing the wheelchair on even a shallow incline. Larger but less obvious social factors also may be present. A homeowners' association might not approve construction of a ramp. A client who feels vulnerable to crime might perceive a ramp as "advertising" the presence of an individual with limited physical skills. The acceptability of a modification depends on the client and others who live in the home and their social and cultural context. Because retrofitting implies that a person or family already calls that structure "home," the occupational therapist must always consider the larger social and cultural context as well as the personal preferences of the client and others who dwell in the home. Because the structure is already home to these individuals and is sited in a neighborhood and community, these less tangible aspects of "fit" often have the greatest impact on the acceptability of proposed modifications. As the occupational therapist considers the activity priorities of the client, the client's performance skills and performance patterns, the therapist also may draw on the principles of universal design to identify modifications that create an acceptable person–environment fit.

■　■　■

Appendix C.
Selected 2004 CPT™ Billing Codes Applicable to Home Modification Practice

In some settings, CPT codes are used to communicate the content of occupational therapy services to a payer. Although there are no CPT codes that are specific to home modifications, the table below identifies CPT codes that may be used appropriately to communicate services related to home modification practice and examples of when each code might be used.

CPT Code	Description of Code	Example of When Code Might Be Used in Home Modification Practice
97003	Occupational therapy evaluation	• Initial occupational therapy evaluation, including assessment of the person–environment fit
97004	Occupational therapy re-evaluation	• Subsequent re-evaluation, including assessment or re-assessment of the person–environment fit
97535	Self-care/home management training (e.g., activities of daily living [ADL] and compensatory training, meal preparation, safety procedures, and instructions in use of assistive technology devices/adaptive equipment), direct one-on-one contact by provider, each 15 minutes	• Direct person–environment assessment in the home subsequent to initial evaluation related to ADL, simple communication device use, home establishment and management, meal preparation and cleanup, and safety procedures and emergency responses • Training in use of modifications for ADL, simple communication devices, home establishment and management, meal preparation and clean-up, and safety procedures and emergency responses
97537	Community and work reintegration training (e.g., shopping, transportation, money management, avocational activities and/or work environment/modification analysis, work task analysis, use of assistive technology device/adaptive equipment), direct one-on-one contact by provider, each 15 minutes	• Direct person–environment assessment in the home subsequent to initial evaluation related to care of others, child rearing, community mobility, financial management, shopping, education, work, and play and leisure • Training in use of modifications for care of others, child rearing, community mobility, financial management, shopping, education, work, and play and leisure
97542	Wheelchair management/propulsion training, each 15 minutes	• Training in controlling or maneuvering a wheelchair in a newly redesigned space or in relation to an access device (e.g., lift, elevator, or ramp)
97755	Assistive technology assessment (e.g., to restore, augment or compensate for existing function, optimize functional tasks and/or maximize environmental accessibility), direct one-on-one contact by provider, with written report, each 15 minutes	• Comprehensive assessment of client performance skills and appropriateness or readiness for modifications and devices subsequent to an initial occupational therapy evaluation. Should be used only in cases in which client's skills are significantly affected and modification needs are complex. Should not be used when alternative communication devices are being assessed or trained.

(continued)

CPT Code	Description of Code	Example of When Code Might Be Used in Home Modification Practice
92605	Evaluation for prescription for non-speech-generating augmentative and alternative communication device	• Comprehensive assessment of client performance skills and appropriateness or readiness for complex non-speech-generating communication device as a home modification
92607	Evaluation for prescription for speech-generating augmentative and alternative communication device, face-to-face with patient; first hour	• Comprehensive assessment of client skills and appropriateness or readiness for complex speech-generating device as a home modification
92608	Each additional 30 minutes (used with 92607)	• Services appropriately coded using 92607, for each 30 minutes beyond the initial hour of service

Note. CPT™ is a trademark of the American Medical Association (AMA). CPT 5-digit codes, nomenclature, and other data are copyright © 2005 by the American Medical Association. All rights reserved. Reprinted with permission. No fee schedules, basic units, relative values, or related listings are included in CPT. The AMA assumes no liability for the data contained herein.

Codes shown refer to CPT 2005. CPT codes are updated annually. New and revised codes become effective January 1. Always refer to annual updated CPT publication for most current codes.

Allowable codes vary by locale, site of service, and payer policy. Payer policy may recognize CPT E&M (99201-99215) to code occupational therapy evaluations.

■ ■ ■

Appendix D.
Preparation and Qualifications of Occupational Therapists and Occupational Therapy Assistants

Who Are Occupational Therapists?

To practice as an occupational therapist, the individual educated in the United States has accomplished the following:

- Graduated from an occupational therapy program accredited by the Accreditation Council for Occupational Therapy Education (ACOTE®) or predecessor organization
- Successfully completed a period of supervised fieldwork experience required by an educational program for occupational therapists that is accredited by ACOTE or predecessor organization.
- Passed a nationally recognized entry-level examination for occupational therapists
- Fulfills state requirements for licensure, certification, or registration

Educational Programs for the Occupational Therapist

These include the following:

- Biological, physical, social, and behavioral sciences
- Basic tenets of occupational therapy
- Occupational therapy theoretical perspectives
- Screening and evaluation
- Formulation and implementation of an intervention plan
- Context of service delivery
- Management of occupational therapy services
- Use of research
- Professional ethics, values, and responsibilities

The fieldwork component of the program is designed to develop competent, entry-level, generalist occupational therapists by providing experience with a variety of clients across the lifespan and in a variety of settings. Fieldwork is integral to the program's curriculum design and includes an in depth experience in delivering occupational therapy services to clients, focusing on the application of purposeful and meaningful occupation and/or research, administration, and management of occupational therapy services. The fieldwork experience is designed to promote clinical reasoning and reflective practice, to transmit the values and beliefs that enable ethical practice, and to develop professionalism and competence in career responsibilities.

Who Are Occupational Therapy Assistants?

To practice as an occupational therapy assistant, the individual educated in the United States has accomplished the following:

- Graduated from an occupational therapy assistant program accredited by the Accreditation Council for Occupational Therapy Education (ACOTE®) or predecessor organization
- Successfully completed a period of supervised fieldwork experience required by an educational program for occupational therapy assistants that is accredited by ACOTE or predecessor organization.
- Passed a nationally recognized entry-level examination for occupational therapy assistants
- Fulfills state requirements for licensure, certification, or registration

Educational Programs for the Occupational Therapy Assistant

These include the following:
- Biological, physical, social, and behavioral sciences
- Basic tenets of occupational therapy
- Screening and assessment
- Intervention and implementation
- Context of service delivery
- Assist in management of occupational therapy services
- Use of professional literature
- Professional ethics, values, and responsibilities

The fieldwork component of the program is designed to develop competent, entry-level, generalist occupational therapy assistants by providing experience with a variety of clients across the lifespan and in a variety of settings. Fieldwork is integral to the program's curriculum design and includes an in depth experience in delivering occupational therapy services to clients, focusing on the application of purposeful and meaningful occupation. The fieldwork experience is designed to promote clinical reasoning appropriate to the occupational therapy assistant role, to transmit the values and beliefs that enable ethical practice, and to develop professionalism and competence in career responsibilities.

Regulation of Occupational Therapy Practice

All occupational therapists and occupational therapy assistants must practice under federal and state law. Currently, 50 states, the District of Columbia, Puerto Rico, and Guam have enacted laws regulating the practice of occupational therapy.

Note. The majority of this information is taken from the *Standards for an Accredited Educational Program for the Occupational Therapist* (AOTA, 1999a), *Standards for an Accredited Educational Program for the Occupational Therapy Assistant* (AOTA, 1999b), and *Standards of Practice* (draft AOTA, 2005).

■ ■ ■

References

AARP. (2000). *Fixing to stay: A national survey on housing and home modification issues.* Washington, DC: Author.

American Occupational Therapy Association. (1979). Uniform terminology for reporting occupational therapy services. *Occupational Therapy News, 35*(11), 1–8 .

American Occupational Therapy Association. (1989). Uniform terminology for occupational therapy (2nd ed.). *American Journal of Occupational Therapy, 43,* 808–815.

American Occupational Therapy Association. (1994). Uniform terminology for occupational therapy (3rd ed.). *American Journal of Occupational Therapy, 48,* 1047–1054.

American Occupational Therapy Association. (1999a). Standards for an Accredited Educational Program for the Occupational Therapist. *American Journal of Occupational Therapy, 53,* 575–582.

American Occupational Therapy Association. (1999b). Standards for an Accredited Educational Program for the Occupational Therapy Assistant. *American Journal of Occupational Therapy, 53,* 583–589.

American Occupational Therapy Association. (2002). Occupational therapy practice framework: Domain and process. *American Journal of Occupational Therapy, 56,* 609–639.

Americans With Disabilities Act, Pub. L. 101-336, 42 CFR 12101 (1990).

Bachner, S. (2000). Objects, physical environment, and self: Implications for home intervention. *OT Practice, 5*(4), 19–22.

Calkins, M. P., & Namazi, K. H. (1991). Caregivers' perceptions of the effectiveness of home modifications for community living adults with dementia. *Journal of Alzheimer's Care and Related Disorder Research, 6*(1), 25–29.

Center for Functional Assessment Research/Uniform Data System for Medical Rehabilitation. (1984). *Guide for the use of the uniform data set for medical rehabilitation.* Buffalo, NY: Author.

Center for Universal Design, North Carolina State University. (1997a). *A blueprint for action: A resource for promoting home modifications.* Raleigh: Author.

Center for Universal Design, North Carolina State University. (1997b). *The principles of universal design* (ver. 2.0). Raleigh: Author.

Close, J., Ellis, M., Hooper, R., Glucksman, E., Jackson, S., & Swift, C. (1999). Prevention of falls in the elderly trial (PROFET): A randomised controlled trial. *Lancet, 353,* 93–97.

Corcoran, M. A., & Gitlin, L. N. (1992). Dementia management: An occupational therapy home-based intervention for caregivers. *American Journal of Occupational Therapy, 46,* 801–808.

Cumming, R. G., Thomas, M., Szonyi, G., Frampton, G., Salkeld, G., & Clemson, L. (2001). Adherence to occupational therapist recommendations for home modifications for falls prevention. *American Journal of Occupational Therapy, 55,* 641–648.

Cumming, R. G., Thomas, M., Szonyi, G., Salkeld, G., O'Neill, E., Westbury, C., et al. (1999). Home visits by an occupational therapist for assessment and modification of environmental hazards: A randomized trial of falls prevention. *Journal of the American Geriatric Society, 47,* 1397–1402.

Fisher, A., & Kielhofner, G. (1995). Skill in occupational performance. In G. Kielhofner (Ed.), *A model of human occupation: Theory and application* (2nd ed., pp. 113–128). Philadelphia: Lippincott Williams & Wilkins.

Gill, T. M., Williams, C. S., & Tinetti, M. E. (2000). Environmental hazards and the risk of nonsyncopal falls in the homes of community-living older persons. *Medical Care, 38,* 1174–1183.

Gitlin, L., Corcoran, M., Winter, L., Boyce, A., & Hauck, W. W. (2001). A randomized, controlled trial of a home environmental intervention: Effect on efficacy and upset in caregivers and on daily function of persons with dementia. *The Gerontologist, 41,* 4–14.

Goffman, E. (1959). *The presentation of self in everyday life.* New York: Doubleday.

Kochera, A. (2002). *Falls among older persons and the role of the home: An analysis of cost, incidence, and potential savings from home modifications.* Washington, DC: AARP Public Policy Institute.

Law, M., Baptiste, S., Carswell, A., McColl, M. A., Polatajko, H., & Pollock, N. (1994). *Canadian Occupational Performance Measure* (2nd ed.). Toronto: Canadian Occupational Therapy Association.

Law, M., Cooper, B., Strong, S., Stewart, D., Rigby, P., & Letts, L. (1996). The person–environment–occupation model: A transactive approach to occupational performance. *Canadian Journal of Occupational Therapy, 63,* 9–23.

Law, M., Polatajko, H., Baptiste, W., & Townsend, E. (1997). Core concepts of occupational therapy. In E. Townsend (Ed.), *Enabling occupation: An occupational therapy perspective.* Ottawa: Canadian Association of Occupational Therapists.

Lawton, M. P. (1980). *Environment and aging.* Monterey, CA: Brooks/Cole.

Mann, W. C., Ottenbacher, K. J., Fraas, L., Tomita, M., & Granger, C. V. (1999). Effectiveness of assistive technology and environmental interventions in maintaining independence and reducing home care costs for the frail elderly. *Archives of Family Medicine, 8,* 210–217.

Mosey, A. C. (1996). *Applied scientific inquiry in the health professions: An epistemological orientation* (2nd ed.). Bethesda, MD: American Occupational Therapy Association.

Parham, L. D., & Fazio, L. S. (Eds.). (1997). *Play in occupational therapy for children.* St. Louis, MO: Mosby.

Pynoos, J., Cohen, E., & Lucas, C. (1988). *The caring home booklet: Environmental coping strategies for Alzheimer's caregivers.* Los Angeles: Long-Term Care National Resource Center, University of California at Los Angles/University of Southern California.

Request for Planning Ideas for the Development of the Children's Health Outcomes Initiative, 66 Fed. Reg. 11296 (2001).

Rogers, J., & Holm, M. (1994). Assessment of self-care. In B. R. Bonder & M. B. Wagner (Eds.), *Functional performance in older adults* (pp. 181–202). Philadelphia: F. A. Davis.

Sanford. J. A. (2004, May). *Definition of home modifications.* Presented at the American Occupational Therapy Association Annual Conference & Expo, Minneapolis, MN.

Stark, S. (2004). Removing environmental barriers in the homes of older adults with disabilities improves occupational performance. *Occupational Therapy Journal of Research, 24,* 32–39.

Toto, P. (2001, December). Building community alliances. *Home and Community Health Special Interest Section Quarterly, 8,* 3–4.

Trombly, C. A. (1995). Occupation: Purposefulness and meaningfulness as therapeutic mechanisms. *American Journal of Occupational Therapy, 49,* 960–972.

World Health Organization. (2001). *International classification of functioning, disability, and health.* Geneva, Switzerland: Author.

■ ■ ■

Selected Reading

American Occupational Therapy Foundation & American Occupational Therapy Association. (1996). *Changing needs, changing homes: A guide to resources.* Bethesda, MD: Authors.

Christianson, M. A. (1990). *Aging in the designed environment.* Binghamton, NY: Haworth Press.

Hammel, J. (2000). Assistive technology and environmental intervention impact on the activity and life roles of aging adults with developmental disabilities: Findings and implications for practice. *Physical and Occupational Therapy in Geriatrics, 18*(1), 37–58.

Mace, R., Hardie, G., & Place, J. (1990). *Accessible environments: Toward universal design.* Raleigh: Center for Universal Design, North Carolina State University.

Marcus, C. C. (1997). *House as a mirror of self: Exploring the deeper meaning of home.* Berkeley, CA: Conari Press.

National Advisory Council on Aging. (1992). *Housing an aging population: Guidelines for development and design.* Ottawa: Government of Canada.

■ ■ ■